Worldly Hopes

By A. R. Ammons

Ommateum
Expressions of Sea Level
Corsons Inlet
Tape for the Turn of the Year
Northfield Poems
Selected Poems
Uplands
Briefings
Collected Poems: 1951–1971
(winner of the National Book Award for Poetry, 1973)
Sphere: The Form of a Motion
(winner of the 1973–1974 Bollingen Prize in Poetry)
Diversifications
The Snow Poems
Highgate Roate
The Selected Poems: 1951–1977
Selected Longer Poems
A Coast of Trees
(winner of the National Book Critics Circle Award for Poetry, 1981)
Worldly Hopes
Lake Effect Country
The Selected Poems: Expanded Edition
Sumerian Vistas
The Really Short Poems
Garbage
(winner of the National Book Award for Poetry, 1993)
Brink Road
Glare

Worldly Hopes

Poems

●●●

A. R. AMMONS

W. W. Norton & Company

NEW YORK ● LONDON

Copyright © 1982 by A. R. Ammons
Reissued as a Norton paperback 2001

Library of Congress Cataloging-in-Publication Data
Ammons, A. R., 1926–
Worldly Hopes : Poems
1. Title.
PS3501.M6W6 811'.54 81-16971
ISBN 0-393-01518-1   AACR2
ISBN 0-393-00081-8 (pbk.)

ISBN 0-393-32185-1 pbk.

W. W. Norton & Company, Inc.,
500 Fifth Avenue, New York, N.Y. 10110
www.wwnorton.com

W. W. Norton & Company Ltd.,
Castle House, 75/76 Wells St., London, W1T 3QT

1 2 3 4 5 6 7 8 9 0

to the memory of Elliott Coleman

Contents

Room Conditioner   1
Extravaganza   2
Righting Wrongs   3
Subsumption   4
Immoderation   5
Vines   6
Extrication   7
Spruce Woods   8
I Went Back   9
Snow Roost   10
Shading Flight In   11
Precious Weak Fields   12
Night Chill   13
Calling   14
Reaction Rates   15
Progress Report   16
Lost & Found   17
Epistemology   19
The Role of Society in the Artist   21
Scribbles   23
Hermit Lark   25
Shit List   27
Limits   30
Sizing   32
Bride   33

Rainy Morning   34
The Scour   35
Meditation   36
Oblivion's Bloom   37
Immortality   38
Design   39
Augmentations in Early March   40
Working Differentials   41
Winter Sanctuaries   42
Cold Spell   43
Planes   44
Volitions   45
Providence   46
Going Without Saying   47
Devastation   48
Merchandise   49
Pairing   50
Rivulose   51

Acknowledgments

I am grateful to the editors of the following periodicals for first publishing the poems listed:

Abraxas—Extravaganza, Shit List
American Poetry Review—Winter Sanctuaries
The Arts Journal—Working Differentials
Beloit Poetry Journal—Immortality, I Went Back
Brim—Pairing, Subsumption
Epoch—Epistemology, The Role of Society in the Artist
Harper's—Limits
The Hudson Review—Design, Spruce Woods
Imprint (Hong Kong)—Hermit Lark
Ocean City Sentinel—Providence
Science 82—Rivulose
Sparrow—Volitions
Tendril—Room Conditioner
Ubu—Righting Wrongs

Worldly Hopes

Room Conditioner

After rain I
walk and looking
down glimpse
the moon: I
back up to see
and the puddle splices
onto two hundred
thousand miles of
height two
hundred thousand
miles of depth

Extravaganza

A leaf picked
up by the
wind could
(if it could)

tell a good
deal about
big affairs, volumes,
currents, long

tugs, ascensions,
wheels quite
truly and be
(dropped by a

ditchhedge) still
nothing
more than a bit of
nothing.

Righting Wrongs

Dew turns
the burgundy smoke
bush ice-white,

puffy airiness
glittering
substance-low:

impatient with dull
wind's and slow sun's
lightenings,

I kicking jar
a shower out, losing,
though, ice for rise.

Subsumption

From
scientific and esthetic
ramblings & bewilderings,
voice, the clearing
through tangled
tone,
will sometimes
just do
something, blow
a leaf off a
branch
without
ambiguity or equivocation
or, a rose,
unwind
into
clarity
simply

Immoderation

If something is too
big, enlarging it
may correct it:

a skinny thing
acquires great force
pushed next to nothing.

Vines

In late August scarlet
fire breaks
out in the spruce top,
a flame flamelike
in disposition but
coal-still
to glow but then,
the spruce holding
green, October comes
and frost flakes fire
off the skinny
highwires of arising.

Extrication

I tangled with
the world to
let it go
but couldn't free

it: so I made
words
to wrestle in my
stead and went

off silent to
the quick flow
of brooks, the
slow flow of stone

Spruce Woods

It's so still
today that a
dipping bough means
a squirrel
has gone through.

I Went Back

I went back
to my old home
and the furrow
of each year
plowed like
surf across
the place had
not washed
memory away.

Snow Roost

Last night the
fluffiest inhabitant
filled the
cedars deep, but this clear
morning windy,
flurries blizzard-thick
explode flight
into local blindings

Shading Flight In

Lit clouds diffuse tree
shadows etiolated long
across the grass-gold winter
lawn, trunks and branches as if
risen aground to a deep
remembrance:
substances—there may not always
be wood, but insubstantial shadow
will always find a solid source.

Precious Weak Fields

Mercy's so slight it's like
a glitter-bit in granite or a single
pane-sun in snow flint or the warp-weave of
slice-light netting a shallows stone.

Night Chill

My big round yew
can stand a gust
into a million
presences: too
many needles
to get through
to get through
except drift through:
birds in there peep and sleep,
puffy in the slow hurry.

Calling

My endorsing song blocks out
to blot out, identifies in keyed
sets and replications,
high rises and office
bldgs, baroque interiors and
mirroring exteriors (spelled out

intricacies) to obliterate into
emptiness, the promise,
cure, commencement, my
self-endorsing song, flattened,
snaking its way out,
reaching to weave into its rise.

Reaction Rates

My hanging strawberry
pot stops drops
geometrically:

I gush water in the
pot top
and because of interior

runoff it
streams through the bottom
hole but

because of interior
absorption stops
rather rapidly

Progress Report

Now I'm
into things

so small
when I

say boo
I disappear

Lost & Found

How I came to
be what I am
I can't unwind

and what's left
from what I
was won't

turn my way
away so I
get upfront

to ongoing

and seek in

the freshwater of
time breaking
into now

the frail
possibilities
of a singular

start, the re-decision
to keep it up, till
now (vanishing)

can become the slice
constantly
standing here.

Epistemology

A bit of
truth
told pops
its pip
and falls
small
into its
(if bitter)

consequence
but the bit
untold
avoided collects
about it
networks
bindings
of disguise &

going
around
till, an
enormous posture,
it can't be
identified
solved or made
to disappear &

so by
recalcitrance &
complication
comes
to represent
the world
truly
ours.

The Role of Society in
the Artist

Society sent me this invitation to go to
hell and
delighted not to be overlooked I thought

I could make arrangements to accommodate
it and went off
where, however, I

did the burning by myself, developing
fortunately some fairly thick shields
against blazing and some games

one of which was verse by which I used
illusion to put the flames out,
turning flares into mirrors

of seeming: society
attracted to this bedazzlement wanted me
to acknowledge how it had been

largely responsible and I said oh yes it gave
me the language by which to send me
clear invitations and society

designated me of social value and lifted me
out of hell so I could better share
paradisal paradigms with it

and it said isn't it generous
of society to let you walk here
far from hell—society does this because

it likes your keen sense of acquired sight
& word: how wonderful of you to say so, I said,
and took some of whatever was being

passed around but every night went out
into the forest to spew fire
that blazoned tree trunks and set

stumps afire and society found me out there
& warmed itself and said it liked my unconventional
verses best & I invited society to go to hell

Scribbles

To unwrite the writing, unweave, ravel out
the woven, unsay the spoken, and make hard
to perceive the seen and known—I go about

to happenstance, loose thread, coincidental
margin and find (if on purpose) by accidence
the brook dimpling shallow through rocks and

think nothing clear on that surface or below
it! and clouds are a fuzzy subject, running
together in flat continuums or breaking

filed away or, best and above it all, simply
dissolving: but the hard writing, the in-chipped
and scrawled, the cut and trenched, that must be

made palimpsest (too much truth already out)
so that the song that is the song of
the hurt and lost cannot emerge through

the singing nor any dark taint light:
someday, I must read the text
but not now, let it not be now, not today

already listing with the grievances of avoidance
but, weatherwise, transparent: or if I am lucky
I will so encushion it with the wires of

verseline, so rustle it with stuttering, or
burn it down with raving, the polish, that failing
sight will miss the failing seen or get no

more from it than a haze of sense: my clear
writing . . . to confuse, subvert, renounce!
my babbling, to make dumb, my light, to hide!

perplexity is such that sometimes it must be
embraced before it will clear, to the deep
clear, when it may be put aside, as a bee

puts aside color, pattern, flight when he reaches
at the stigma's base the pure nectar:
as I may put writing aside someday to seek to know.

Hermit Lark

Shy lark! I'll bet it took a while to get you
perfect, your song quintessential, hermit lark,
just back from wherever you winter: I learn my real

and ideal self from you, the right to sing
alone without shame!
water over stone makes useless brook music; your

music unbearably clear after rain
drops water breaking through air, the dusk air
like shaded brookwater, substanced clarity!

I learn from you and lose the edginess I speak of
to one other only, my mate, my long beloved, and
make a shield not so much against the world,

though against its hardest usages, as
for tenderness's small leeways: how
hard to find the bird in the song! the music

breaks in from any height or depth of the spiral
and whirling up or down, jamming, where does it
leave off: shy bird, welcome home, I love your

song and keep my distance: hold, as I know you
won't, through the summer this early close visitation
behind the garage and in the nearby brush:

you will pair off and hiding find deeper
shyness yet: be what you must and will be:
I listen and look to found your like in me.

Shit List; or,
Omnium-gatherum of
Diversity into Unity

You'll rejoice at how many kinds of shit there are:
gosling shit (which J. Williams said something
was as green as), fish shit (the generality), trout

shit, rainbow trout shit (for the nice), mullet shit,
sand dab shit, casual sloth shit, elephant shit
(awesome as process or payload), wildebeest shit,

horse shit (a favorite), caterpillar shit (so many dark
kinds, neatly pelleted as mint seed), baby rhinoceros
shit, splashy jaybird shit, mockingbird shit

(dive-bombed with the aim of song), robin shit that
oozes white down lawnchairs or down roots under roosts,
chicken shit and chicken mite shit, pelican shit, gannet

shit (wholesome guano), fly shit (periodic), cockatoo
shit, dog shit (past catalog or assimilation),
cricket shit, elk (high plains) shit, and

tiny scribbled little shrew shit, whale shit (what
a sight, deep assumption), mandril shit (blazing
blast off), weasel shit (wiles' waste), gazelle shit,

magpie shit (total protein), tiger shit (too acid
to contemplate), moray eel and manta ray shit, eerie
shark shit, earthworm shit (a soilure), crab shit,

wolf shit upon the germicidal ice, snake shit, giraffe
shit that accelerates, secretary bird shit, turtle
shit suspension invites, remora shit slightly in

advance of the shark shit, hornet shit (difficult to
assess), camel shit that slaps the ghastly dry
siliceous, frog shit, beetle shit, bat shit (the

marmoreal), contemptible cat shit, penguin shit,
hermit crab shit, prairie hen shit, cougar shit, eagle
shit (high totem stuff), buffalo shit (hardly less

lofty), otter shit, beaver shit (from the animal of
alluvial dreams)—a vast ordure is a broken down
cloaca—macaw shit, alligator shit (that floats the Nile

along), louse shit, macaque, koala, and coati shit,
antelope shit, chuck-will's-widow shit, alpaca shit
(very high stuff), gooney bird shit, chigger shit, bull

shit (the classic), caribou shit, rasbora, python, and
razorbill shit, scorpion shit, man shit, laswing
fly larva shit, chipmunk shit, other-worldly wallaby

shit, gopher shit (or broke), platypus shit, aardvark
shit, spider shit, kangaroo and peccary shit, guanaco
shit, dolphin shit, aphid shit, baboon shit (that leopards

induce), albatross shit, red-headed woodpecker (nine
inches long) shit, tern shit, hedgehog shit, panda shit,
seahorse shit, and the shit of the wasteful gallinule.

Limits

Since the
unknown's
truer
than the
known

and since

mystery
can
make a well-known weed
unreal

and since

bent we
break on
time that lets
everything endure
changed

why not take
liberties
and love
what is not

storm the intangible
for the lore
song's lost in

Sizing

Some ideas hit
brush too thick
to mingle through
or clearings
too wide to bound

Bride

for Minfong Ho

Sometimes a maple seed
can hold on so
tight it spins
way out on the wind strong
enough to snap it free!

Rainy Morning

Sometimes the ridge across
the way transluminous
emerges above the mist
and squares and detached rondures
of vapory ground with
dairy barns and old trees
break out afloat
separated in high lyings

The Scour

It was so windy
last night the snow
got down nowhere
except against something.

Meditation

Spot fires rifle the woods
and gold and scarlet
flash hilltop to hill,
hedgerows and fields waylaid giving
way: the sky drops ash
to cover the gone
or spent and the long
build up of white
takes care of everything.

Oblivion's Bloom

Struck head to
ground in
first cold
the bumblebee
turns
in the sweetest
nectar yet

Immortality

The double lanceolate
needlelike
hemlock leaf

will, falling, catch on
a twitch of old
worm-silk

and, like a fall worm,
dingledangle breezy
all day in the noose

Design

The drop seeps whole
from boulder-lichen
or ledge moss and drops,

joining, to trickle,
run, fall, dash,
sprawl in held deeps,

to rush shallows, spill
thin through heights,
but then, edging,

to eddy aside, nothing
of all but nothing's
curl of motion spent.

Augmentations in
Early March

The grail trees this
morning are
ice-corseted to the least
twig and a breeze,
sun-raised,
squeaks the got-up skeletons
limb against limb
with music frazzled
multiple as mist
settling or as treesful
of gritty grackles
on their way here now.

Working Differentials

The mts,
their pushy
roundness,
force
streams
to wind
but the streams
to wind less
take the
roundness
away and
put it down
flat
where they
though then
meander deeply
as if at
leisure or in
spite.

Winter Sanctuaries

The squirrel, bunching branches,
knits a billowing raft
from twigends and, riding air, lifts
one paw to pull in a tip
where shaken maple seed cling.

Cold Spell

The sun seeps the evergreens'
long-wood shade
off the snow and the cut
of light deepens into ditchbanks;

hedgerows (gray clatter) trap
windy heat-holdings, and barns,
fences stall the perpendicular:
even the fretwork of

old vines, too skinny for snow,
radiates a filigree
of the caught let go and
zero gives up by noon to one.

Planes

The whirlwind lifts
sand to
hide holy
spun
emptiness or erect a
tall announcement
where formed
emptiness is to be found

Volitions

The wind turned
me round and
round all day, so
cold it planed
me, quick it

polished me
down: a spindle
by dusk,
too lean to
bear the open dark,

I said, sky,
drive me
into the
ground here,
still me with the ground.

Providence

To stay
bright as
if just
thought of
earth requires
only that
nothing stay

Going Without Saying

What to make of a breeze—
a spruce bough in
large measure nods:
maple leaves flicker

or break (go) out with
sparse wobbles: poplars
as in shivering loft
shake flip-side bright

and rattle glistering
mix's wind and light:
willow sheathes seep the air
unjangling through.

Devastation

When possibility fell
from many to one
to none

the place I stood in widened:
but the Way I
thought is without extent

and can empty emptiness
emptier
and fill earth and sky

with the abundance of
its absence and stand beside
me, a neighbor.

Merchandise

When we have
played with
the toy life

death takes it
back without
condition

whatever the condition

Pairing

Wish is a closer
rightness

than reason which
wish

tosses into careful
resistances to

be obtained:
but when

wish is not to be
wished

reason like a
failed mate

roams the woods
of the self

whining for the
lost one

Rivulose

You think the ridge hills flowing, breaking
with ups and downs will, though,
building constancy into the black foreground

for each sunset, hold on to you, if dreams
wander, give reality recurrence enough to keep
an image clear, but then you realize, time

going on, that time's residual like the last
ice age's cool still in the rocks, averaged
maybe with the cool of the age before, that

not only are you not being held onto but where
else could time do so well without you,
what is your time where so much time is saved?